Table Of Contents

Chapter 1: Introduction to Louisiana LLC Setup   1

  Understanding the Basics of an LLC   1

    Benefits of Forming an LLC in Louisiana   3

    Overview of the 24-Hour Setup Process   5

Chapter 2: Preparing for Your Louisiana LLC   8

  Choosing a Name for Your LLC   8

  Reserving Your LLC Name (Optional Step)   9

  Selecting a Registered Agent   11

Chapter 3: Obtaining an EIN   14

  Applying for an EIN from the IRS   14

Chapter 4: Filing Your Articles of Organization   16

  Completing the Required Forms   16

Chapter 5: Creating an Operating Agreement   18

Importance of an Operating Agreement   18

Drafting Your Operating Agreement   19

Chapter 6: Business Licenses and Tax Obligations for Your New LLC   22

Researching and Obtaining Necessary Business Licenses   22

Understanding Tax Obligations for Your LLC   24

Chapter 7: Opening a Business Bank Account   26

Choosing the Right Bank for Your LLC   26

Setting Up Your Business Bank Account   28

Chapter 8: Maintaining Compliance for Your Louisiana LLC   30

Annual Reporting Requirements   30

Tax Filing Requirements   32

Staying Up to Date with Louisiana LLC Laws   33

Chapter 9: Expanding Your Louisiana LLC   36

Hiring Employees and Independent Contractors   36

Protecting Your LLC with Proper Insurance Coverage   38

Exploring Growth Opportunities for Your Business   40

Chapter 10: Conclusion and Next Steps   42

Reviewing Your Louisiana LLC Setup Process   42

Planning for the Future of Your Business   44

Seeking Professional Help When Needed   46

Chapter 1: Introduction to Louisiana LLC Setup

Understanding the Basics of an LLC

For entrepreneurs and small business owners looking to set up a Louisiana LLC in just 24 hours or less, it is essential to understand the basics of what an LLC is and how it operates. An LLC, or Limited Liability Company, is a popular business structure that combines the flexibility and tax benefits of a partnership with the liability protection of a corporation.

One of the key advantages of forming an LLC is that it offers limited liability protection to its owners, known as members. This means that the personal assets of the members are typically shielded from the debts and liabilities of the business. In the event of a lawsuit or bankruptcy, the members' personal assets are generally not at risk.

Another benefit of an LLC is its pass-through taxation structure. This means that the profits and losses of the business are passed through to the individual members, who report them on their personal tax returns. This can result in tax savings for the members, as they may be able to take advantage of certain deductions and credits not available to corporations.

In addition, an LLC offers flexibility in terms of management and ownership structure. Members can choose to manage the business themselves or appoint a manager to oversee day-to-day operations. They can also decide how the profits and losses will be allocated among the members, allowing for a customized approach to ownership.

Overall, understanding the basics of an LLC is crucial for entrepreneurs and small business owners looking to establish a Louisiana LLC quickly and efficiently. By taking advantage of the benefits of limited liability protection, pass-through taxation, and flexibility in management and ownership, individuals can set themselves up for success in their business endeavors.

Benefits of Forming an LLC in Louisiana

Forming a Limited Liability Company (LLC) in Louisiana offers numerous benefits for entrepreneurs and small business owners looking to establish a strong legal foundation for their business. Here are some of the key advantages of choosing to form an LLC in Louisiana:

1. Limited Liability Protection: One of the most significant benefits of forming an LLC is the limited liability protection it provides to the owners. This means that the personal assets of the owners are protected from any business debts or liabilities, reducing the risk of financial loss in case of legal issues or bankruptcy.

2. Tax Benefits: LLCs in Louisiana are considered pass-through entities for tax purposes, which means that the profits and losses of the business are reported on the owners' personal tax returns.

This can result in potential tax savings for small business owners, as they may be able to take advantage of deductions and credits that are not available to other business structures.

3. Flexibility in Management: LLCs offer flexibility in terms of management structure, allowing owners to choose how they want to run their business. Whether you prefer a member-managed LLC where all owners have a say in the day-to-day operations, or a manager-managed LLC where designated individuals handle management responsibilities, you have the freedom to customize the management structure to suit your needs.

4. Credibility and Professionalism: By forming an LLC, you demonstrate to customers, clients, and vendors that you are serious about your business and are committed to operating in a professional and transparent manner.

This can help build trust and credibility with stakeholders, leading to increased opportunities for growth and success.

Overall, forming an LLC in Louisiana offers a range of benefits for entrepreneurs and small business owners, including limited liability protection, tax advantages, flexibility in management, and enhanced credibility. By taking advantage of these benefits, you can establish a solid legal foundation for your business and set yourself up for long-term success.

Overview of the 24-Hour Setup Process

This subchapter will provide an overview of the 24-hour setup process for forming a Louisiana LLC. For entrepreneurs and small business owners looking to establish their business quickly and efficiently, this step-by-step guide will walk you through the necessary procedures to set up your LLC in just one day.

The first step in the 24-hour setup process is to choose a unique name for your LLC that complies with Louisiana's naming requirements. You will need to conduct a name search to ensure that your desired name is available and not already in use by another business entity.

Next, you will need to appoint a registered agent for your LLC. A registered agent is responsible for receiving legal documents and official correspondence on behalf of your business. You can choose to appoint yourself as the registered agent or hire a professional registered agent service.

After selecting a name and registered agent, you will need to obtain an Employer Identification Number (EIN) from the Internal Revenue Service (IRS). An EIN is required for tax purposes and allows you to open a business bank account and hire employees.

Once your EIN is obtained, you can file Articles of Organization with the Louisiana Secretary of State.

This document officially establishes your LLC and includes key information such as the name of your business, your registered agent's address, and the LLC members' names.

Finally, you will need to create an operating agreement for your LLC, outlining the ownership and management structure of the business.

While not required by law, an operating agreement is essential for clarifying the rights and responsibilities of LLC members and can help prevent disputes in the future.

By following this overview of the 24-hour setup process, entrepreneurs and small business owners can quickly and efficiently establish their Louisiana LLC and begin operating their business in just **one day**!

It is important to emphasize that to establish your Louisiana LLC within 24 hours or less, it is crucial to leverage all available online resources. Opting out of utilizing online options can significantly prolong the process, potentially extending it to several weeks or even months.

Chapter 2: Preparing for Your Louisiana LLC

Choosing a Name for Your LLC

Choosing a name for your LLC is an important step in setting up your business. Your LLC's name is not only how customers will identify your brand, but it also plays a crucial role in the legal and administrative aspects of your business. When selecting a name for your Louisiana LLC, several factors must be considered.

First and foremost, your LLC's name must comply with Louisiana's naming guidelines. The name must include the words "Limited Liability Company" or the abbreviation "LLC." Additionally, the name must be distinguishable from the names of existing businesses in Louisiana.

You can check the availability of your desired name by searching the Louisiana Secretary of State's online database online at www.sos.la.gov in the "Business Services" section.

When choosing a name for your LLC, it's important to pick a name that is unique, memorable, and reflective of your brand. Consider the industry you are in, your target audience and the image you want to portray. Avoid using generic names that do not stand out or are too similar to existing businesses.

It's also a good idea to conduct a trademark search to ensure that your chosen name is not already trademarked by another business. This will help you avoid potential legal issues down the line.

In conclusion, choosing a name for your Louisiana LLC is a crucial decision that requires careful consideration. By following the guidelines outlined above, you can select a name that will help your business stand out and succeed in the competitive market.

Reserving Your LLC Name (Optional Step)

This step is completely optional.

Before filing your new LLC's articles of organization with the Louisiana Secretary of State, you have the option of reserving a unique name for your business. The name of your LLC is important as it will be how customers identify and recognize your brand. If you want to ensure that your desired name is available and not already in use by another business, you can reserve it with the Louisiana Secretary of State.

To reserve your LLC name, you will need to conduct a name search on the Louisiana Secretary of State's website to check for availability. Once you have confirmed that your desired name is unique, you can then proceed to reserve it by filing a Name Reservation Request with the Secretary of State's office via their website at www.sos.la.gov.

It is important to note that reserving your LLC name does not automatically register your business entity.

It simply gives you the exclusive right to use that name for a period of time while you complete the necessary steps to formally establish your LLC.

The reservation of your LLC name is valid for 60 days, during which time you must file your Articles of Organization to officially register your business entity. If you fail to do so within 60 days, your reserved name will become available for others to use.

By reserving your LLC name early in the process, you can ensure that your desired business name is secure and not taken by another entity.

Selecting a Registered Agent

Selecting a Registered Agent is a crucial step when setting up your Louisiana LLC. A Registered Agent is a designated individual or company responsible for receiving legal documents, tax notices, and other important correspondence on behalf of your LLC.

Choosing the right Registered Agent can have a significant impact on the success and compliance of your business.

When selecting a Registered Agent for your Louisiana LLC, several factors must be considered. First and foremost, your Registered Agent must have a physical address in Louisiana where they can be reached during regular business hours. This is important to ensure that important documents are received in a timely manner.

Additionally, your Registered Agent should be reliable, trustworthy, and experienced in handling legal and business matters. They should also have a good understanding of the local laws and regulations that govern LLCs in Louisiana. This will help ensure that your business remains in good standing with the state and that any legal issues are handled promptly and effectively.

It is also important to consider the cost of hiring a Registered Agent. While some entrepreneurs may choose to serve as their own Registered Agent to save money, it is often worth the investment to hire a professional service. This can help you avoid potential legal pitfalls and ensure that your business runs smoothly.

In conclusion, selecting a Registered Agent is a critical decision when setting up your Louisiana LLC. By choosing a reliable and experienced professional, you can rest assured that your business will be well-equipped to handle any legal challenges that may arise.

Chapter 3: Obtaining an EIN

Applying for an EIN from the IRS

If you're an entrepreneur or small business owner looking to set up a Louisiana LLC in just 24 hours, one of the crucial steps in the process is applying for an Employer Identification Number (EIN) from the IRS. An EIN is essentially a social security number for your business, allowing you to open a business bank account, hire employees, and file taxes.

To apply for an EIN, you can do so online through the IRS website at www.IRS.gov. The process is relatively straightforward and can be completed in just a few minutes. You'll need to provide information about your business, such as the name, address, and type of business entity. You'll also need to provide your personal information as the responsible party for the business.

Once you've submitted your application online, you'll receive your EIN immediately, allowing you to continue with the process of setting up your Louisiana LLC in 24 hours. Make sure to keep your EIN in a safe place, as you'll need it for various business activities moving forward.

Having an EIN is not only necessary for legal and tax purposes but also adds credibility to your business. It shows that you are serious about your business and have taken the necessary steps to establish it properly.

By following these steps and applying for an EIN from the IRS, you'll be well on your way to setting up a Louisiana LLC in just 24 hours. This is an essential aspect of starting your business on the right foot and ensuring its success in the long run.

Chapter 4: Filing Your Articles of Organization

Completing the Required Forms

As an entrepreneur or small business owner looking to set up your Louisiana LLC in just 24 hours, completing the required forms is a crucial step in the process. By ensuring that all the necessary paperwork is filled out accurately and submitted on time, you can expedite the formation of your LLC and start operating your business sooner.

One of the most important forms you will need to complete is the Articles of Organization. This document officially registers your LLC with the state of Louisiana and provides essential information about your business, such as its name, address, purpose, and members. Filling out this form correctly is key to ensuring that your LLC is legally recognized and compliant with state regulations.

To ensure that your LLC is set up in 24 hours, this step must be completed online via the Louisiana Secretary of State's website at www.sos.la.gov. Please note that the Secretary of State requires a filing fee and a convenience fee to file your Articles of Organization.

Before submitting your form online, make sure to double-check all the information you have provided. Ensure that all the required fields are filled out correctly. Any errors or missing information could delay the processing of your application.

Please note that each registered agent for the business will be required to respond to an email from the Secretary of State before the Articles of Organization will be approved. Please ensure that you provide an accurate email address for all registered agents.

By following these steps, you can ensure that your Louisiana LLC is officially registered and ready to start operating. Remember to keep copies of all your paperwork for your records and consult with a legal professional if you have any questions about the registration process.

Chapter 5: Creating an Operating Agreement

Importance of an Operating Agreement

One of the most crucial elements of forming a Louisiana LLC is creating an operating agreement. This document outlines the ownership and operating procedures of your business, and it is essential for protecting your interests and ensuring smooth operations.

For entrepreneurs and small business owners in Louisiana, having an operating agreement in place is key to establishing clear guidelines for decision-making, profit-sharing, and dispute resolution. Without this document, your LLC may be subject to the default rules set forth by state law, which may not align with your specific business needs and goals.

An operating agreement helps to clearly define the roles and responsibilities of each member of the LLC, as well as the procedures for adding or removing members.

It also outlines how profits and losses will be distributed among members, setting expectations and avoiding potential conflicts down the line.

Furthermore, having an operating agreement in place can help protect your limited liability status. By clearly delineating the separation between your personal assets and those of the LLC, you can shield yourself from personal liability in case of legal disputes or financial challenges.

Overall, an operating agreement provides a solid foundation for your Louisiana LLC, ensuring that all members are on the same page and working towards the same goals. By taking the time to create this document, you are setting your business up for success and minimizing the risk of potential conflicts or legal issues in the future.

Drafting Your Operating Agreement

When drafting your operating agreement, there are several key components to consider.

Firstly, you will need to outline the ownership structure of the LLC, including the percentage of ownership each member holds. This will help clarify each member's financial stake in the business and their voting rights on important decisions.

Additionally, your operating agreement should address how profits and losses will be allocated among members, as well as how any future changes in ownership will be handled. This can help prevent disputes over financial matters and ensure that all members are on the same page regarding the financial health of the business.

Furthermore, your operating agreement should outline the management structure of the LLC, including the roles and responsibilities of each member. This can help prevent confusion over who is in charge of day-to-day operations and ensure that tasks are delegated efficiently.

Overall, drafting a comprehensive operating agreement is crucial for the success of your Louisiana LLC.

By clearly outlining the rules and regulations that govern your business, you can prevent conflicts and set the stage for a successful and harmonious business venture. Take the time to carefully consider each component of your operating agreement to ensure that your LLC is set up for success.

Chapter 6: Business Licenses and Tax Obligations for Your New LLC

Researching and Obtaining Necessary Business Licenses

Researching and obtaining necessary business licenses is a crucial step in setting up your Louisiana LLC. As entrepreneurs and small business owners, it is important to understand the legal requirements and regulations in order to operate your business smoothly and avoid any legal issues.

Before starting the process of obtaining business licenses, it is essential to conduct thorough research to determine which licenses are required for your specific type of business in Louisiana. This may vary depending on the nature of your business, location, and industry. You can start by visiting the Louisiana Secretary of State website or contacting the Louisiana Department of Revenue for more information.

Once you have identified the necessary licenses for your Louisiana LLC, the next step is to gather all the required documentation and information. This may include your LLC formation documents, proof of insurance, zoning permits, and any other relevant paperwork. Make sure to double-check the requirements to avoid any delays in the licensing process.

When applying for business licenses, it is important to follow the instructions carefully and submit all the necessary paperwork in a timely manner. Keep track of the application process and follow up with the appropriate authorities if needed.

Remember that obtaining the necessary business licenses is not only a legal requirement but also a way to establish credibility and trust with your customers. By being proactive and thorough in researching and obtaining the required licenses, you are setting your Louisiana LLC up for success in the long run.

Understanding Tax Obligations for Your LLC

As an entrepreneur or small business owner in Louisiana, understanding your tax obligations for your Limited Liability Company (LLC) is crucial to maintaining compliance with state regulations and maximizing your financial success. In this subchapter, we will break down the key tax considerations for LLCs in Louisiana, providing you with the knowledge and tools necessary to navigate this aspect of your business with confidence.

One of the primary advantages of forming an LLC in Louisiana is the flexibility it offers in terms of taxation. LLCs are considered pass-through entities, meaning that profits and losses are passed through to the owners, who report them on their personal tax returns. This can result in significant tax savings, as LLCs are not subject to corporate income tax at the state level.

However, it is important to note that LLCs are still responsible for certain taxes at the state and federal levels.

In Louisiana, LLCs are required to pay an annual franchise tax, which is based on the net worth of the company. Additionally, LLC members are subject to self-employment taxes on their share of the company's profits.

To ensure that you are meeting all of your tax obligations as an LLC owner in Louisiana, it is highly recommended to consult with a qualified tax professional. They can help you understand your specific tax requirements, maximize your deductions, and develop a tax strategy that aligns with your business goals.

By taking the time to educate yourself on the tax obligations for your LLC, you can avoid costly mistakes and position your business for long-term success. Remember, staying informed and proactive when it comes to taxes is key to protecting your bottom line and maintaining compliance with state regulations.

Chapter 7: Opening a Business Bank Account

Choosing the Right Bank for Your LLC

When starting a business in Louisiana, one of the most crucial decisions you will make is choosing the right bank for your LLC. The bank you select will be responsible for handling your business finances, processing transactions, and providing you with the necessary financial tools to help your business grow. Here are some key factors to consider when choosing the right bank for your LLC.

First and foremost, you should look for a bank that offers business accounts specifically designed for LLCs. These accounts typically come with features that cater to the needs of small businesses, such as low fees, online banking options, and easy integration with accounting software.

It is also important to consider the location and accessibility of the bank's branches and ATMs. You want to choose a bank that is conveniently located near your business or home, so you can easily access your funds and speak with a representative if needed.

Another crucial factor to consider is the bank's reputation and customer service. Look for a bank that has a good track record of working with small businesses and providing excellent customer service. You want a bank that is responsive to your needs and can provide you with personalized support when necessary.

Additionally, consider the fees and charges associated with the bank's services. Make sure you understand the fees for maintaining your account, processing transactions, and any other services you may need. Choose a bank that offers competitive rates and transparent fee structures.

By taking the time to research and compare different banks, you can find the right financial partner for your LLC.

A good bank will not only help you manage your finances more effectively but also support your business growth and success.

Setting Up Your Business Bank Account

Setting up a business bank account is a crucial step in establishing your Louisiana LLC. Not only does it separate your personal and business finances, but it also adds a layer of professionalism to your company. In this subchapter, we will guide you through the process of setting up your business bank account in just a few simple steps.

Once you have selected a bank, you will need to gather the necessary documentation to open your business bank account.

This typically includes your LLC formation documents from the Secretary of State, your EIN (Employer Identification Number) from the IRS, and your personal identification. Some banks may also require additional documents, so be sure to check with your chosen institution beforehand.

Next, you will need to deposit the initial funds into your business bank account. This amount will vary depending on the bank and the type of account you choose. Be sure to keep detailed records of this transaction for tax and accounting purposes.

After you have completed these steps, you are ready to start using your business bank account for all of your financial transactions. Remember to keep your personal and business finances separate to maintain the liability protection offered by your LLC.

By following these simple steps, you can quickly and easily set up your business bank account and take the next step towards building a successful Louisiana LLC.

Chapter 8: Maintaining Compliance for Your Louisiana LLC

Annual Reporting Requirements

As an entrepreneur or small business owner in Louisiana, it is crucial to understand the annual reporting requirements for your LLC. Failing to comply with these requirements can result in penalties and potential business disruptions. This subchapter will guide you through the necessary steps to ensure that your Louisiana LLC remains in good standing with the state.

The Louisiana Secretary of State requires all LLCs to file an annual report by a specific deadline each year. This report provides updated information about your business, such as the names and addresses of members, managers, and registered agents. It also ensures that your LLC's contact information is current and accurate.

Failure to file the annual report on time can result in late fees and, ultimately, the administrative dissolution of your LLC. To avoid these consequences, it is essential to mark your calendar with the annual report deadline and set reminders well in advance. This will give you ample time to gather the necessary information and submit the report on time.

In addition to the annual report, Louisiana LLCs must also maintain accurate financial records and comply with any tax reporting requirements. Keeping detailed records of your business's income, expenses, and profits will not only help you stay organized but also ensure that you are prepared for tax season.

By staying on top of your annual reporting requirements, you can protect your LLC's good standing and focus on growing your business. Remember, compliance is key to a successful business venture in Louisiana.

Tax Filing Requirements

As an entrepreneur or small business owner in Louisiana, it is crucial to have a clear understanding of your tax obligations to ensure compliance with state and federal laws. Failure to meet your tax responsibilities can result in penalties, fines, and even legal action. In this section, we will discuss the key tax obligations that you need to be aware of when setting up and operating your Louisiana LLC.

Next, you will need to determine the type of taxes your Louisiana LLC is required to pay. This may include federal income tax, state income tax, sales tax, and payroll taxes. It is important to consult with a tax professional to ensure you are correctly calculating and remitting the appropriate taxes.

In Louisiana, LLCs are subject to a state income tax rate of 4% on net income. Additionally, businesses in Louisiana are required to collect and remit sales tax on taxable goods and services.

Understanding your sales tax obligations and properly collecting and remitting these taxes is crucial to avoid costly penalties.

Finally, it is essential to keep accurate and organized financial records to support your tax filings. This includes maintaining records of income, expenses, deductions, and receipts. By staying organized and informed about your tax obligations, you can avoid potential issues and focus on growing your Louisiana LLC successfully.

Staying Up to Date with Louisiana LLC Laws

As an entrepreneur or small business owner in Louisiana, it is crucial to stay up to date with the constantly changing laws and regulations that govern LLCs in the state. By staying informed, you can ensure that your business remains compliant and avoid any potential legal issues that may arise.

One of the best ways to stay current on Louisiana LLC laws is to regularly check the Louisiana Secretary of State website for any updates or changes to the regulations.

The Secretary of State's office is responsible for overseeing the formation and registration of LLCs in the state, so any new laws or regulations will be posted on their website.

Additionally, it is a good idea to consult with a legal professional who specializes in business law to help you navigate the complex legal landscape surrounding LLCs in Louisiana. An attorney can provide you with valuable insights and advice on how to ensure that your business remains in compliance with all applicable laws and regulations.

Finally, networking with other entrepreneurs and small business owners in Louisiana can also be a valuable resource for staying up to date with LLC laws. By joining local business groups or attending industry events, you can stay informed about any changes to the laws that may impact your business.

In conclusion, staying up to date with Louisiana LLC laws is essential for ensuring the success and longevity of your business.

By taking proactive steps to stay informed and seek professional advice when needed, you can protect your business and avoid any potential legal pitfalls.

Chapter 9: Expanding Your Louisiana LLC

Hiring Employees and Independent Contractors

When starting a business in Louisiana, one of the most important decisions you will have to make is whether to hire employees or independent contractors. Each option has its own set of benefits and drawbacks, so it is crucial to understand the differences before making a decision.

Hiring employees can be a great way to build a dedicated team that is committed to the success of your business. Employees typically work set hours and are managed directly by you, giving you more control over their work. However, hiring employees also comes with added responsibilities, such as paying payroll taxes, providing benefits, and adhering to labor laws.

On the other hand, hiring independent contractors can be a more flexible and cost-effective option for small businesses. Independent contractors are self-employed individuals who work on a project-by-project basis. They are responsible for their own taxes and benefits, which can save you time and money. However, working with independent contractors also means less control over their work and schedules.

Before making a decision, it is important to carefully consider your business needs and the specific roles you are looking to fill. If you need a long-term, dedicated team member, hiring an employee may be the best choice. On the other hand, if you need specialized skills for a short-term project, working with an independent contractor may be more suitable.

Regardless of which option you choose, it is important to clearly outline the terms of the agreement in a written contract. This will help prevent misunderstandings and protect both parties in case of disputes. Additionally, make sure to familiarize yourself with Louisiana labor laws and regulations to ensure compliance with state requirements.

Overall, the decision to hire employees or independent contractors will depend on your business needs, budget, and goals. By carefully weighing the pros and cons of each option, you can make an informed decision that will benefit your business in the long run.

Protecting Your LLC with Proper Insurance Coverage

As an entrepreneur or small business owner in Louisiana, setting up your LLC in just 24 hours is a great accomplishment. However, once your business is up and running, it's crucial to protect it with the right insurance coverage. Insurance can provide financial security and peace of mind in the event of unexpected events, such as accidents, lawsuits, or natural disasters.

One of the most important types of insurance for your LLC is general liability insurance. This type of insurance protects your business from third-party claims of bodily injury, property damage, or personal injury. It can cover legal fees, medical expenses, and settlements, helping to prevent financial ruin in the face of a lawsuit.

Another important form of insurance is property insurance, which covers the physical assets of your business, such as equipment, inventory, and buildings. This type of insurance can protect your business from losses due to theft, fire, vandalism, or other covered perils.

If your LLC has employees, you may also need workers' compensation insurance, which provides benefits to employees who are injured or become ill on the job. This type of insurance is required by law in Louisiana and can help protect your business from costly lawsuits and medical expenses.

In addition to these basic types of insurance, many other types of coverage may be beneficial for your LLC, depending on the nature of your business. These may include professional liability insurance, cyber liability insurance, and commercial auto insurance.

By investing in the right insurance coverage for your LLC, you can protect your business from financial risks and ensure its long-term success. Remember, it's always better to be prepared for the unexpected than to be caught off guard.

Exploring Growth Opportunities for Your Business

In this subchapter, we will delve into the various growth opportunities available for your Louisiana LLC. As an entrepreneur or small business owner, it is important to constantly seek out ways to expand and improve your business. By exploring different avenues for growth, you can ensure the long-term success and sustainability of your company.

One of the first steps in exploring growth opportunities for your business is to conduct a thorough analysis of your current market and industry. By understanding the trends, challenges, and opportunities in your specific niche, you can identify areas where your business can grow and thrive. This market research will also help you identify potential competitors and develop strategies to differentiate your business and attract new customers.

Another important growth opportunity for your Louisiana LLC is to diversify your product or service offerings.

By expanding your range of products or services, you can appeal to a wider customer base and increase your revenue streams. This could involve introducing new products, entering new markets, or offering additional services to your existing customers.

Additionally, exploring strategic partnerships and collaborations can be a valuable growth opportunity for your business. By partnering with other companies or organizations, you can leverage their expertise, resources, and customer base to reach new markets and expand your business. Collaborations can also provide opportunities for innovation and product development, helping you stay ahead of the competition.

Overall, by actively seeking out growth opportunities and being open to new ideas and partnerships, you can ensure the continued success and growth of your Louisiana LLC. With careful planning and strategic decision-making, you can take your business to the next level and achieve your long-term goals.

Chapter 10: Conclusion and Next Steps

Reviewing Your Louisiana LLC Setup Process

Now that you have successfully completed the setup process for your Louisiana LLC in just 24 hours, it is important to take some time to review and reflect on the steps you have taken. This will not only help you ensure that everything has been done correctly, but also give you a better understanding of how your LLC is structured and what your responsibilities are as a business owner.

The first thing to review is the paperwork that you have filed with the Louisiana Secretary of State. Make sure that all the information is accurate and up to date, including your LLC name, registered agent, and member or manager details. Double-checking these details will help you avoid any potential issues in the future.

Next, review your Operating Agreement. This document outlines the ownership and management structure of your LLC, as well as the rights and responsibilities of each member. Make sure that the Operating Agreement reflects the agreements you have made with your business partners and that it aligns with your long-term goals for the company.

Finally, review your tax obligations as an LLC in Louisiana. Make sure that you understand the state and federal tax requirements for your business, including sales tax, income tax, and any other applicable taxes. Keeping up to date with your tax obligations will help you avoid penalties and ensure that your business remains in good standing with the authorities.

By taking the time to review your Louisiana LLC setup process, you can feel confident that your business is on the right track and set up for success. Remember, setting up an LLC is just the first step – it is important to continuously review and update your business practices to ensure long-term success.

Planning for the Future of Your Business

Planning for the future of your business is crucial to ensure its long-term success and sustainability. As entrepreneurs and small business owners in Louisiana, setting up an LLC in just 24 hours is just the first step. Now, it's time to focus on strategic planning to secure the future of your business.

One key aspect of planning for the future of your business is setting clear and achievable goals. Define what you want to achieve with your business in the short-term and long-term, and develop a roadmap to reach those goals. This will help you stay focused and motivated as you work towards building a successful business.

Another important aspect of planning for the future of your business is financial planning. This includes creating a budget, managing cash flow, and setting aside funds for future investments or emergencies.

By keeping a close eye on your finances and planning ahead, you can avoid financial pitfalls and ensure the financial health of your business.

Furthermore, it's essential to continuously evaluate and adapt your business strategy to changing market conditions and trends. Stay informed about industry developments, monitor your competitors, and be prepared to pivot if necessary. Flexibility and adaptability are key to staying ahead in the competitive business landscape.

In conclusion, planning for the future of your business is essential for long-term success. By setting clear goals, managing your finances effectively, and staying adaptable to market changes, you can secure the future of your Louisiana LLC and build a thriving business that stands the test of time.

Seeking Professional Help When Needed

As an entrepreneur or small business owner setting up your Louisiana LLC in just 24 hours, it's important to know when to seek professional help.

While the process may seem straightforward, some intricacies and legalities can easily trip you up if you're not careful. That's why knowing when to turn to experts for guidance can save you time, money, and potential headaches down the road.

One area where professional help is often needed is in legal matters. Setting up an LLC involves navigating through various state regulations, tax laws, and business requirements. A qualified attorney can help ensure that your LLC is set up correctly and that you are in compliance with all relevant laws and regulations. They can also provide valuable advice on protecting your personal assets and minimizing liability.

Another area where professional help may be necessary is in accounting and tax preparation. A certified public accountant (CPA) can help you set up your LLC's financial systems, track expenses, and ensure that you are paying the correct amount of taxes. They can also provide valuable advice on tax deductions and credits that can save you money in the long run.

Finally, seeking professional help when it comes to marketing and branding can also be beneficial. A marketing consultant can help you develop a solid marketing strategy, create a strong brand identity, and reach your target audience effectively. They can also provide valuable insights on social media marketing, advertising, and other promotional tactics to help your business grow.

In conclusion, knowing when to seek professional help is a key aspect of setting up your Louisiana LLC in 24 hours. By turning to experts in legal, accounting, and marketing fields, you can ensure that your business is set up for success from the start. Don't be afraid to ask for help when you need it – it could make all the difference in the long run.